Getting to Know
India

Illustrated by KATHLEEN ELGIN

Getting to know
INDIA

by BARNETT D. LASCHEVER

FREDERICK MULLER LIMITED · LONDON

First published in Great Britain in 1961 by
Frederick Muller Limited

Printed in Great Britain by Jarrold & Sons Ltd, Norwich

© 1960 by COWARD-McCANN, INC.

Author, illustrator, and publisher wish to acknowledge with appreciation the courtesy and assistance given by Miss Hira Nirodi, Mrs. Shireen Subramanya and Mr. Saeed Jaffrey in checking the manuscript for factual information.

TO MOTHER
for her understanding and inspiration

A LONG TIME AGO, the people of India believe, there was a demon with ten heads. His name was Ravan. He stole into India from the island of Ceylon and carried off Sita, the queen of India's good King Rama.

In despair King Rama called on his fine friend Hanuman, the Monkey King, for help. The Monkey King and his monkey army, together with King Rama, attacked Ceylon. In a furious battle they beat the evil Ravan and rescued the queen.

If you visit India in late September or early October, you can see people still celebrating that famous victory of the good kings

over the forces of evil. The celebration is called the Dashahara Festival. It lasts for ten days. On the last day giant paste-board figures representing Ravan and his evil brothers are put up on a fair-ground.

The figures are as high as a house. Inside are fireworks. As night falls, flaming arrows are shot into the figures by an actor playing King Rama. The fireworks explode and Ravan and his brothers burst into flames. The crowd cheers as the demons are destroyed. Actors dressed as King Rama and his friend King Hanuman re-enact the old story on stages throughout the country, for Dashahara is one of the most popular holidays in India.

Perhaps you wonder why Indians believe in a story about a monkey army helping a man king. In India, the visitor from the Western world finds much that seems mysterious and strange.

Indians who come to our country think some of our customs are strange, too. They find it difficult to understand Father Christmas. But they do not laugh at the big fat man in a red suit with a long white beard who comes down the chimney in the middle of the night with toys. We do not need to laugh at a monkey king.

This story of India is about a civilization that goes back 5,000 years. Yet, as an independent country, India is very young.

Only in 1947 did she become independent after more than 200 years of British rule. Earlier, in the fifteenth, sixteenth and seventeenth centuries, British, Portuguese and Dutch traders came to India. The British stayed on and made India a part of their vast empire. Those were times when many European nations had colonies. In modern times, two new independent countries were created from the old India. India was for Hindus. Pakistan was formed for Moslems. These are the two biggest religions of the region. Not all Moslems of the region live in Pakistan today, however. There are still 40,000,000 in India.

The Moslems are one of many different groups who came to ancient India. These groups all pushed their way in because India is a land bridge between the Orient and the Middle East. India's northern borders are a 1,500-mile-long wall of the world's highest

9

mountains, the Himalayas. On the west India is bordered by West Pakistan and on the east by East Pakistan. The northern half of India lies between the two sections of that nation.

To the north-east, beyond the Himalayas, lie Nepal, Tibet and China. The southern half of India is a huge peninsula shaped like an upside-down triangle. On the west of the triangle is the Arabian Sea. On the east lies the Bay of Bengal, and off the tip is the Indian Ocean.

Travelling from the northern mountains to the southern tip, you would go from near-Arctic cold to tropical heat. You could explore a desert, then dense jungles, flat plains of farmland, great forests of sandalwood, satinwood and teak, orchards of date and coconut palms.

In the earliest days a dark-skinned people called Dravidians lived in India. Then a light-brown people called Aryans conquered the Dravidians and made them slaves. Aryan legends and beliefs became the foundation of Hinduism.

The early Hindus organized life in what became known as the caste system. They classified people according to their position in life.

The highest class, or caste, was the Brahmans. They were teachers and priests. They believed they were the best of all Hindus. The lowest caste was the Untouchables. They were descended from the conquered Dravidians.

The Untouchables had to do all the dirty work. When cows

China

Afghanistan

Kashmir

Srinagar

Tibet

West
Pakistan

Himalaya Mountains

Delhi
New Delhi

Nepal

Allahabad
Benares

Jumna R.

Ganges River

East Pakistan

Calcutta

INDIA

Burma

Bombay

Jaipur

Bay of
Bengal

Madras

Arabian Sea

Ceylon

Indian Ocean

died in the fields, the Untouchables had to take the carcasses away. They cleaned the places used for lavatories and swept the streets.

"Don't touch me!" a Hindu would cry to a man, dusty from sweeping. The fear of touching is how the name "Untouchable" arose. Some Hindus even feared they had been made unclean if they so much as came into the shadow of an Untouchable.

As time passed, India gained a reputation for being a very rich country. When Columbus discovered America he was really hunting for the riches of India. Like others before him, he had been lured by tales of fabulous cities and temples.

One of the most famous men to seek India's treasures was Alexander the Great. He came from a part of northern Greece known as Macedonia. After he had conquered near-by countries, he tried to conquer India too. With his mighty army he pushed his way through the mountains into India. Here at last the great warrior was stopped.

India was too vast for him. He died of fever while trying to go home.

Next to come to India were traders from Arabia and Afghans from Afghanistan. With them, they brought the Moslem religion.

At first not many Indians became Moslems. Then the Moghuls came to India from Persia. They too were Moslems, and the religion grew. The Moghuls also brought new forms of poetry, art and architecture.

You can still visit the beautiful monuments they built. The most famous is the Taj Mahal. A Moghul emperor, Shah Jahan, ordered it as a tomb for his beloved wife. It took 20,000 workers seventeen years to finish it. Today its white marble walls still twinkle and shine with jewels, inlaid long ago. Four slender towers with domed tops mark the four corners of the tomb.

All round is a garden. A long sunken pool, fed by bubbling fountains, leads from the garden gate to the Taj. Many people like to get their first sight of the Taj when the moonlight glistens on the white marble and the silver fountains. Only by daylight, though, can you read the ninety-nine different names for God which the Shah had engraved on the tomb.

In modern India, it's easy to recognize Moghul architecture. The buildings have graceful curves, tall spires, high arches and lattice screens of marble. The screens are like lace carved in stone. Pictures of flowers and trees are made with jewels, instead of paint. There are never any pictures of the human figure in holy buildings, because the Moslem religion forbids it.

Moslem beliefs were laid down by the prophet Mohammed. They are written in the holy book, the Koran. Moslems worship one God whom they call Allah. Five times a day, they kneel and pray to him, no matter where they are.

Moslems also practise fasting.

They believe doing without food and drink gives them strength and courage. During their month of Ramadan they eat and drink only after sunset and just before the sun comes up. Forty days after the end of Ramadan, Moslems celebrate Id-uz-zuha. That holiday is in honour of the time when Abraham was going to sacrifice his son, Isaac. In the Old Testament book of Genesis you can read how God stopped Abraham and told him to sacrifice a ram, instead of his son.

Abraham was the founder of the Hebrew religion, and a father of Christianity. Moslems respect him, too. They also respect Moses and Jesus.

Hindus speak of many Gods. Some say there are 330,000,000 Hindu gods. Actually there is only one: Brahma, the creator. All the others are reincarnations of that one.

To a Hindu, reincarnation means that if a person lives a good and righteous life, after he dies his soul will enter the body of a new-born baby. This next life will be happier than the former one.

Hindus also believe the souls of evil people will suffer in the bodies they enter in the next life. Worst of all, the soul may enter the body of an animal. A very bad person may become an ass or a jackal.

God, too, they think is reincarnated on earth in different forms. The two most important are Vishnu, the preserver, and Shiva, the destroyer. One of the popular reincarnations of Vishnu is the good King Rama. But most popular of all throughout India is Lord Krishna, the eighth reincarnation of Vishnu.

Lord Krishna is a very handsome god. He is a favourite with the girls. As a child he was full of mischief and liked to play tricks on his mother and on the *gopis*.

Gopis are milkmaids. Once the child Krishna stole their clothes while they were swimming. Another time he and a friend stole his mother's butter. Then there was the time during Holi when he threw coloured water on the gopis. That was all right because Holi is a holiday announcing the coming of spring. It's the custom for everyone to put on old clothes and go about splashing coloured water on their friends.

When Lord Krishna grew up, he left his home and the gopis who loved him. He became the charioteer for a mighty warrior, Arjuna. Together they fought the great battle of Kurukshetra.

The battle represented the fight between good and evil. Arjuna lifted his great bow but suddenly he couldn't fight. Although his side was right, Arjuna couldn't bear the thought of killing other human beings. It was then that Lord Krishna spoke to him.

He spoke of love, and brotherhood and God. He spoke of pleasure and pain, and of death. Lord Krishna talked for many hours while the armies waited. Finally, he told Arjuna that good men must always fight against evil. So Arjuna lifted his bow once more and let fly with an arrow. The battle raged. At the end, Arjuna and his army triumphed.

The words and teachings of Lord Krishna were put down in the *Bhagavad Gita*. This is the Bible of Hinduism.

There are many statues of Lord Krishna and other incarnations of God in Hindu temples. Some have four arms, others many faces. To the Hindu, the extra arms mean that God has great strength. The extra heads mean He has great wisdom.

Faith in the strength and wisdom of his God helped a gentle little Hindu to lead Indians to freedom. In the early part of our century, Mahatma Gandhi began his work. Like Arjuna, he had an argument with himself. He wanted India free of British rule, but he did not want to kill the rulers. He led his people in a movement that became known as "passive resistance". Gandhi told the people not to fight with weapons, not to hurt and kill. Instead they were not to obey their rulers' instructions and orders. They refused to do anything the British told them. They lay down on the railway tracks to stop trains. They fasted. They prayed. They refused to buy British goods. But they were never abusive. They never lifted a hand in anger. Passive resistance finally won independence for India.

People in South Africa who disliked the government's policy of *apartheid* tried Gandhi's method. In America, college students have practised passive resistance as a means of winning equal opportunities for their Negro and white friends.

When passive resistance helped to bring India independence, its leaders decided the Untouchables should enjoy it too. They were the people who were treated the worst. One of the first laws passed in the new republic abolished the Untouchable caste. Gandhi gave Untouchables a new name—Harijans, children of God.

Although Indian law says no one is an Untouchable, some people refuse to obey. They still refuse to let Harijans enter their temples or to give them good jobs. We have a similar problem in our country. Although all citizens have equal rights and perhaps we think we have no colour bar, it is often difficult for coloured people to get lodgings and decent jobs. It's the same in India.

While India was trying to solve its problems as a new nation, a terrible thing happened. Gandhi was murdered by an assassin. Not only his countrymen but the whole world mourned. He will always be remembered by the Indians and by many other people, too, as one of the greatest men who ever lived.

Gandhi once said: "I do not want a kingdom, salvation or heaven; what I want is to remove the troubles of the oppressed and the poor."

He had good reason to be upset about the poor in his country.

There are so many of them. Most of them go to bed hungry every night. Those who live in the cities may sleep in the streets. Those who live in the country may have mud huts to sleep in. India is a crowded country—she has 400,000,000 people. You may say this is not so crowded as Britain, because although India has about eight times as many people as Great Britain she has roughly thirteen times as much land. But Britain is largely an industrial country, while India is an agricultural one. This means India needs more land for each person. As a result, few Indians eat well or have fine houses in cities like Bombay, New Delhi, Calcutta and Madras.

These cities are a combination of old and new. New Delhi has a separate section called Old Delhi. Riding along the marine drive which circles Bombay's harbour you can look out at modern sea-going freighters, or inland to the fragile spires of ancient temples.

Most Indians, however, don't live in cities. They are farmers. Watching an Indian farmer at work, you discover several reasons why so many Indians have so little to eat.

The first reason is that a farmer works only a small patch of land at a time. He moves his oxen and plough from patch to patch. He plants and harvests the same way.

This tending the land in patches is called "fragmentation farming". Sometimes the patches one farmer works are far apart. Taking care of them is much harder and costs more than farming one big connected area. Time and again, the farmer has to stop and move his tools. It's difficult for him to water separated fields, too. Sometimes he gets into family quarrels over using the well water and over whose fields the water ditches may cross.

Fragmentation farming came about because of an old law. The law says that when a Hindu dies, his sons can divide his land in equal parts and each son may take a piece. Since each son always wants a piece of the best land, he gets a bit of it here and a bit of it there. When he dies his children divide his pieces the same way.

Visiting an Indian village with a boy who lives there, you can discover a second reason why farmers don't grow enough food to feed all the people.

Ram, your host, takes you to his hut. You meet his sister Shalu. She is busy patting cow dung into cakes. She sticks the cakes on the outside walls of the house, to dry in the sun. The dung ought to be put back into the fields where it would fertilize the soil and make more crops grow. The trouble is that most Indian villagers can't afford wood to burn in their small clay stoves, so they use dried dung. It burns well.

Some Indian factories make chemical fertilizer, but there isn't nearly enough to go round yet. Besides, most farmers are too poor to buy it. So what could be used to grow more crops is used instead to cook the little that grows.

In Ram's village, you'll come across a third important reason why India can't grow enough food. There isn't enough water.

Ram will take you to a deep well at the edge of town. Two oxen go round and round the well, pulling poles attached to their yokes. The poles operate a pump that brings up a little water each time the oxen go round. The water falls into an irrigation ditch and flows to the crops.

Sometimes the wells dry up. Then famine strikes the land. Even though in some of India's thick jungles there are 426 inches of rain a year, the rain there does the farmers no good. They live on flat plains where there may be no more than 2 inches of rain a year.

In the dry season, everything withers. Even the weeds turn brown and ugly. No longer can children hear the tinkle of running water in the brooks. These, too, are brown and dry.

The sun scorches the earth. It beats down on the mud-hut villages. Hot wind swirls the dust. It fills people's lungs and eyes. They cough and cry. It's so hot, it's impossible to work. Everything slows down. People slow down, cattle slow down. Even the chattering monkeys become still in the heat of the afternoon. Everyone prays for the monsoon, the heavy rains.

The monsoon season usually starts in June. The farmers watch the brilliant blue sky for the first sign of a rain cloud.

They watch with anxious hearts. No sign. Then—look—there it is! There on the horizon is a small dark cloud. It grows bigger and bigger and is joined by others. Soon the sun is blotted out. The sky is heavy with rain clouds.

The first drops fall. The farmers cry out in joyful thanksgiving. The parched earth soaks up the first showers. Then the clouds pour out life-giving waters. Soon, purple, red and yellow wild flowers will bloom in the green fields. The land will come to life again. The crops will grow.

To help Indians survive the times when the monsoon is not good, the government is building many huge dams. Water from good monsoons and from rivers collects behind the dams and forms lakes.

The water in these lakes is then led off into irrigation ditches. It flows to fields for many miles around. Farmers in the area can water their crops all the year, not just during the monsoon season. The dams also help to control floods when the monsoon is too heavy. Too heavy a monsoon can bring as much disaster as none at all. It can ruin crops, wash villages away and drown people.

The dams not only control rain from the monsoons. They also supply India with electric power. The power is used in the many new factories built since the country became independent. At the bases of the dams are machines that make electricity. Water stored behind the dams falls through big pipes. When it hits the machines, it forces them to produce the electric current.

It's a far cry from one of these big power dams to the little ox-driven well in Ram's village. Nevertheless, the well means life to his village. After he has shown it to you, he may invite you home for supper. The meal will be meagre. You'll probably wonder how his family manages to live on so little.

The truth is sad. They probably won't live long. They work too hard and eat too little to have long lives.

Your Indian village meal will start with *dal*, which is lentils.

In your honour, the dal will be covered with fried onions. Ram's Mother has fried them in ghee, a butter made from the milk of cows, water buffalo or goats. Since Ram's Mother has no refrigerator, she has boiled the butter. That keeps it from spoiling.

Shalu, Ram's sister, has sliced cucumbers, long and thin. She spices them with black pepper. She and Ram are more interested in the pudding, however. It is made from jaggery, a thick brown molasses. Peanuts, sesame seeds or coconut are stirred into the molasses. Then the mixture is rounded into little balls.

It is much sweeter than anything you have ever tasted. If you don't like it, you can have fruit instead: bananas, mangoes, or pomegranates. The egg-shaped mango is yellowish-red in colour. Be careful it doesn't squirt all over you! It's full of juice.

If you choose pomegranate, tear off the thick skin to reach the many seeds buried in the pulp. From the seeds you suck a tart liquid something like currant juice.

In different Indian homes, you would discover many new tastes and customs. Food differs, depending on where your hosts live, and what their religion is. In a Moslem home, you may have beef, but never any pork. A belief that pork isn't clean grew up in the ancient world because people became ill after eating it. Pork won't keep long without ice and of course there weren't any refrigerators in the old days. There still aren't many in India, so the rule is still good.

In a Hindu home, families eat all kinds of vegetables, but no meat at all. The Hindu religion forbids all meat. The vegetables are served in a curried sauce, hot as red pepper. In southern India, the curried vegetables are served with rice. In the north, they are served with home-baked *roti* or *chapati*. Roti is a thick bread and chapati, a thin, round one. Both are brown and taste a bit like pie-crust.

The bread comes in handy to help to pick up your food because, except in big cities, Indians don't use knives or forks. Some don't use plates, either. They serve food on the clean leaves of banana trees.

After you finished supper at Ram's house, the banana leaves would be thrown away. Then Ram might ask you to join his friends in a game of Kabaddi. Children play it all over India. Two teams oppose each other across a line drawn in the dirt.

The first contestant takes a deep breath. "Kabaddi, kabaddi, kabaddi," he says, over and over again. At the same time he dashes across the line and tries to touch one of the enemy. If he succeeds, the boy he touches is out of the game. Meanwhile, the other team tries to capture the boy who crossed the line. The idea is to hold him until he runs out of breath and stops saying "Kabaddi". He isn't allowed to take a second breath and if he stops saying the magic word, he's out of the game, too.

The fun continues until only one boy is left. His team wins. Only if you are a boy, will you play with Ram and his friends. Boys and girls don't play together in India. They don't go to parties together, either. When they are old enough to marry, their parents arrange their marriage. Only in the big cities do young people choose their own sweethearts. Their parents' choices seem to work well for them, though. Their family life is happy.

Little girls have happy times among themselves. If you're a girl, Shalu will teach you the game of Uchee-Zameen, Neechi-Zameen. This means "Highland-Lowland". The game is like tag. If you climb on a rock or hump of land, you're "safe". If you jump off, you may be chased and tagged by the girl who is "it".

After the games are over, the villagers may gather to watch a group put on a play.

Probably they'll dramatize a tale from the great Hindu epic, *Ramayana*. As the name suggests, it's the life story of the good King Rama. Yes, everyone shouts, we want the story of Rama and Hanuman, the Monkey King.

As the actors get ready, the excited villagers talk and laugh. When the sky turns dusky grey, one of them throws a torch on a pile of wood.

"O-o-o-h," gasps the crowd as the sparks rise in a golden fountain through the leaves of the trees.

Now there is a hush as the first actor comes forth. Everyone watches intently, for Indians never tire of this story. As the good Rama and Hanuman charge against the bad Ravan, they swing and chop with their mighty swords. The crowd cheers and so do you.

After the play, the villagers dance. Each part of the country has a different way of dancing. The Bharata Natyam in southern India is usually performed by one dancer at a time. The dancer moves eyes and hands as well as feet. Her gestures are considered the purest form of Indian dancing.

After the dance ends Ram cries out: "Let's sing for our British friends." Everyone joins in a tune that sounds as though a few notes were being repeated over and over again. Listen closely. It isn't quite the same each time. Actually, the singers are repeating the main theme in different ways.

When the singing is over, you go back to the cool, dark mud hut of your friend. You'll probably sleep on a mat, spread on the hard-packed dirt floor. If your friend is richer than most villagers, you may sleep on a mattress woven from rope and attached to a frame.

Out in the jungle an elephant trumpets. Flying foxes swoop through the lichee trees. A pack of jackals howls around the village until someone scares them away. Their noise awakens a brain-fever bird in a mango tree. He sings like a nightingale.

Next morning the villagers greet a procession of holy men. The whole village goes out to welcome them. There are thousands of holy men in India. They are called *swamis* or *sadhus*. Some wear flowing, draped, mustard-coloured robes. Others wear only a small cloth round their waists. Some have three horizontal white stripes on their foreheads. They are followers of Shiva, the destroyer. Others have three vertical stripes. They are followers of Vishnu, the preserver. Many are hermits. They live in caves and spend most of their lives thinking about God.

The name of one holy man is well known in India today—
Vinoba Bhave. He and his followers walked about the country and
asked people who owned much land to give some of it to the poor
peasants who had none. Hundreds of thousands of acres have been
given to the peasants because Vinoba Bhave begged for them.

Once a year millions of people follow the holy men of India in
a pilgrimage to the city of Allahabad. Here the Jumna and Ganges
rivers meet. To Indians these rivers are sacred. A mythical river,
the Saraswati, is supposed to join them from the centre of the
earth. This holy spot is known as Triveni—a trinity of rivers. On
the night and the morning of the dark of the moon, a tremendous
gathering of pilgrims from all India crowds into the Ganges.
There they bathe to celebrate the defeat of fierce demons by incarnations of their God.

The whole of the Ganges River is sacred to Indians. It is par-
ticularly sacred, though, where it passes the holy city of Benares.
Benares is a metropolis of temples. The temples line the river
banks for almost four miles.

Steps lead down to *ghats* and then to the water. A ghat is a plat-
form on the river-banks. Sadhus stand on the ghats. They face
straight into the sun and pray. If they keep this up long enough,
the intense light blinds some of them.

Some platforms are "burning" ghats. Fortunate are the Hindus
whose dead bodies are burned on these ghats. Their ashes are

sprinkled in the sacred Ganges. Hindus believe the souls of those whose ashes go into the Ganges don't have to enter any more bodies. They can live forever in heaven.

Walking along the river-bank in Benares, you may share the path with a cow or two. Cows are allowed to walk on the streets and pavements of India. Sometimes they sit down in the middle of the road and stop traffic. No one must harm them because Hindus believe they are sacred.

The belief grew up because butter, ghee and cheese are all made from cow's milk. In the early days, these were the only foods the people had. The cows were life-givers.

Because cows are not killed, India has more of them than almost any other place in the world. India also has more monkeys because they, too, are sacred. You can often see them hanging in the trees as you drive along a country road. When you remember the story of the Monkey King, you can understand why monkeys are revered.

The cows and monkeys are sacred only to the Hindus, however. There are many more Hindus than members of other religions, but there are many other religions, too. Two of them, Buddhism and Jainism, began in India.

Only a few miles from Benares, a monument marks the spot where Prince Gautama Buddha delivered his first sermon. He gave up being a prince to start Buddhism. He taught that if you love your neighbour, God will love you too.

About the same time that Buddha was preaching, Lord Mahavira was teaching the Jainist belief that God loves the soul of every living thing—even an insect. Jains won't kill even a mosquito. Very religious Jains sweep the path before them as they walk, to avoid stepping on any soul God loves.

Besides the Jains, Buddhists, Hindus and Moslems, there are four other kinds of worshippers. If you see a bearded Indian wearing a turban and carrying a dagger, he is probably a Sikh. The Sikhs are just the opposite of the gentle Jains. They have a reputation for being tough, brave warriors.

It may surprise you that 8,500,000 Indians are Christians. During the life of Christ, one of his disciples, Saint Thomas, travelled to southern India. He was welcomed and allowed by the local Hindu king to convert people.

From Persia came the ancient religion of Zoroastrianism. Its followers in modern India are called Parsees. There are also followers of Judaism.

Indians, you see, have many ways of worship. They have many ways of speaking, too.

Southern Indians speak a different language from those in the north. The southerners are descended from Dravidians, the original people of India. Most of them speak Tamil.

In the north, Hindus speak Hindi. Moslems speak Urdu. And these languages are only the beginning. Fourteen main ones are spoken in all, each with several dialects. Fortunately, English is also spoken by Indians who studied it in school when their country was ruled by Britain. Now English helps the people to understand each other. Today, all schoolchildren study Hindi, the official language, along with their regional one.

Thirty million children go to Indian schools. There aren't nearly enough schools yet, though the government is building them as fast as it can. The scarcity of buildings is one reason why many Indian children have school outdoors. Another reason may be

that they like to study under the trees. Classes may meet in the shade of a *peepul* tree or beneath the sword-like leaves of the *neem* tree. Children know ghosts are supposed to live in the oak-like peepul tree. Before school starts, they can peel a sliver of bark from the neem tree, and use it to brush their teeth. It has a strong taste, and serves as brush and paste all in one.

Some of the children of Srinigar, capital of the Indian state of Kashmir, go to school on a river. Imagine having classes on a boat! The gondola-shaped *shikara* is tied at the banks of the river Jhelum. Sometimes the school hoists anchor and sails down the river to the beautiful gardens of Shalimar. Here fountains built by Moghuls long ago still sparkle over beds of red, orange and yellow flowers.

On land or water, pupils study the same subjects all over India. They learn to read and write. They learn the geography and history of their country. When they tackle arithmetic, their teacher tells them that the system of counting now used throughout the world was first invented in India. So was the use of the figure zero.

Children are trained at school to use their hands as well as their heads. They are taught carpentry, weaving and handicrafts. Where there are schools, attendance is compulsory until a child is fourteen. Only a small number go on through secondary schools—they are called "high schools"—to one of India's 534 colleges and universities.

The world over, students love a holiday. Republic Day, on January 26th, is India's national one. It celebrates the country's birth as a new nation. People from every region come to the capital city of New Delhi to show off their local dances and watch the big parades.

There are many holidays kept by different religions in India, too. Divali, like our Christmas, comes at the beginning of winter. Flames from little clay lamps and candles twinkle a welcome in doorways and on the roofs and window ledges of village homes. In the cities, buildings are outlined with strings of electric bulbs. People exchange presents and children get sweets.

Divali is the time when new crops are planted and merchants begin a new year of business. The festival honours Lakshmi, a Hindu goddess who represents the Supreme Being's concern for man's prosperity.

From old beliefs, Indian children learn ideals that help them to look with courage and hope towards the future. Although three-quarters of their parents are farmers, young people want India to become an industrial nation. Already, some of them work in factories that are busy making aeroplanes. Others work in plants that make locomotives, tractors and lorries. Indian factories also turn out cement, matches, chemicals, paper and leather goods. They make iron, coal and steel into useful products.

How to make more products faster is the business of Indian scientists. They are working in fourteen different laboratories. In one of these, in Bombay, scientists are experimenting with isotopes. These are radio-active particles, like those given off by an atom bomb. The Indians are trying to work out how to use them to run factory machines, grow more food, heal the sick.

This work is part of what the Indian government calls "Five-Year Plans".

When India was born as an independent nation, it decided the best way to grow up was to look ahead five years at a time. It set targets to reach every five years, just as though you made a mark on the wall and said: "Five years from now I will be as tall as this." The Indian people look up towards these five-year targets and try to produce enough from factories and farms to reach them.

They produce not only for themselves, but also for other countries. When they sell abroad what they make, they earn more money. One popular product abroad is yak tails. The yak is a furry animal which lives in Ladakh, high in the Himalayan mountains, near India's northern border. His tail makes the best Father Christmas beard in the world.

For centuries, Ladakh was separated from the rest of the world by mountains. Its people were astonished when modern inventions came over the mountains. When the first aeroplane landed, they tried to feed it hay!

All over India, there are villages where people are just beginning to learn what happens in the outside world.

When the monsoon is good, village farmers grow rice and wheat for their families. They grow much of the tea we drink. They raise some of the peanuts which are mashed into your peanut butter. Whole families harvest the peanut vines. The peanuts are clustered at the roots, so the plant must be pulled up to get the nuts.

In some of the country villages, people also weave beautifully patterned cloth on hand looms. The most handsome of all cloths is used in the Indian *sari*.

This is the national costume of the Indian woman. It is all one piece of material, six yards long. Saris come in striking colours, brilliant blues, black embroidered with gold, shimmering white and scarlet embroidered with silver. Women drape their saris to suit themselves. Generally, though, they begin by tucking one end into a half-slip. Then they start winding round from head to foot. As they wind they make some pleats, but leave at least two yards free to flutter. When they have finished, they toss the loose end over the left shoulder, or over the head like a hood. A woman in a sari doesn't seem to walk—she seems to flow.

The trousers of Indian men aren't so glamorous as women's saris. The national trousers of India are the *dhoti*. The dhoti is a long, wide strip of white cotton. It's wrapped round the waist

and between the legs. It looks like a big baby's napkin. It may not be glamorous but it's light, airy, comfortable and easy to wash.

The dhoti is worn mostly by country people. In cities, many men wear white duck trousers.

Actually, there are almost as many different kinds of costumes in India as there are languages. The best way to see the various costumes is to visit a bazaar. You can travel to it in a *tonga*, a horse-drawn, two-wheeled cart with back-to-back seats.

The bazaar, in a street or market place, is crowded with merchants and customers. There's a bustle of people coming and going. They wear turbans, jungle helmets, tunics, saris, white trousers, dhotis, pyjamas. Some wear *phirans*—long flowing robes. Some just wrap themselves in an old piece of cloth. Little children often scurry about with no clothes at all.

Shoppers bargain earnestly. They offer the merchant a lower price than he asks. He shouts, "Oh, I am losing money, but since you are such a gentleman, you can have it for less." He names a

price a little bit lower. The buyer shakes his head. "Still too much," he says. Finally, the two of them agree on a price.

Bargaining is a great game. The merchant wouldn't have any fun if a customer paid the first price he asked.

The air of the bazaar is strong with the scent of spices and flowers like sweet jasmine—and perhaps old fish, too. Fish, flowers, fruit, vegetables, jewellery; saris and sandals; cigarettes and teacups;

beds and bicycles—a bazaar sells just about everything you can imagine

There is always a crowd round the betel nut vendor. He sells betel nuts and a lime powder, along with little round leaves. Indians wrap the nut and powder in the leaf and chew the mixture, just as some people chew chewing-gum. It turns red in their mouths. The pavement and streets of the bazaar are often splattered with red marks. That's where the nut chewers have spat out the juice.

Another popular man in the bazaar is the bangle seller. Indian women wear three or four bangles on each arm. For only a few pennies, they can buy the newest kinds.

Next to the bangle booth is a stall where copper and brass trays glint in the sunlight. In front of the trays are statuettes of dancing Hindu gods. Here indeed are the treasures of the Orient.

A jeweller may beckon you into his shop. At first there is no talk of buying or money. A servant brings tea. You speak of the weather, and where you come from. When the talk finally gets down to business, the jeweller spreads out for your choice his topazes, garnets, emeralds and zircons. It's hard to make up your mind, because they all glisten and glitter, each with a different fire.

49

Perhaps you'll even see a snake-charmer in the bazaar. He opens a round basket. Then he plays a sorrowful-sounding tune on his flute. Slowly a big cobra in the basket uncoils itself and lifts its head. The music continues to wail. The snake raises itself up, swaying all the while to the snake-charmer's tune.

The tonga cart that takes you to and from the bazaar seems primitive compared with India's modern aeroplanes in which visitors can fly all over the country. An overnight ride on an Indian train would seem even stranger than a tonga trip.

Travellers on Indian trains bring their own bedrolls to use in their berths. The compartments often hold four and sometimes eight people. It makes no difference if your travelling companions are strangers, they are so friendly you'll enjoy talking with them.

At first you may think they are getting too personal. They ask many questions. Don't be upset. It's considered polite when strangers meet in India for each to ask the other such questions as: "How old are you?" "Where do you live?" "What do you do?"

The Indian will expect you to ask him the same kind of question. Indians feel it's much easier to talk to each other after they learn these personal facts.

A train trip through India is likely to take you through a princely state. Before India became independent it had many rich princes. They were called *maharajahs*, and *nawabs*, or *nabobs*. The maharajahs were Hindu. The nawabs, or nabobs, were Moslems.

They had royal-sounding names like the Maharajah of Cooch-Behar or the Nawab of Bhopal.

These rulers owned most of the land in their princely states. They were very rich and built magnificent palaces. They owned many elephants. They drove fast, expensive cars.

For amusement they hunted tigers in the jungle or staged big parades. Through the streets of their capital cities they would ride their elephants. The elephants were decked with ribbons and feathers, just as they are in a circus. (The Queen and Prince Philip went on a tiger hunt and rode on elephants during their tour of India in 1961.)

But the princes' parades did not make the people happy. They were desperately poor because they had to pay the princes such high taxes to keep the elephants and cars and palaces.

When India became independent most of the land was taken away from the princes. It was divided up and given to the families who had been working on it so long. The princely states became regular states in the new Republic of India. The princes were given annual salaries, but not big ones. Most of them could no longer afford elephants and palaces. Some have turned their palaces into hotels. If you visit the city of Jaipur you can sleep in a hotel that was once the palace of the Maharajah. Jaipur is called the pink city, because most of the buildings in town are built of pink stone.

As soon as the Indian people were free from the rule of the British and their own princes, they chose to have a democratic republic. The head of the republic is the Prime Minister. Jawaharlal Nehru is a name everyone will remember as a great and troubled Indian Prime Minister. He was elected after Gandhi was murdered, and he had to face almost as much trouble as Gandhi did.

This time, the trouble came from Communist China. The dictator of that country sent armies into countries on India's northern borders, then into India itself. Like Arjuna at the battle of Kurukshetra, and like Gandhi, Nehru didn't want Indians to fight and kill. Indians try to be friends with all people. Their country is a member of the United Nations.

But what should they do about people who *start* a fight? As in the long wait at Kurukshetra, Indians are taking time to decide.

Besides the Prime Minister, the other most important part of the Indian government is its parliament. The parliament has two parts, like the British Houses of Parliament. One part is the Rajya Sabha—Council of States; the other the Lok Sabha—House of People. Members of the Council of States are elected by legislatures of the fourteen Indian states. The people choose their representatives in the House of People.

All citizens can vote as soon as they are twenty-one. Because not all voters can read, the ballots have pictures instead of names. Different parties use different pictures—often of animals. The voter chooses by making his mark next to the picture he knows belongs to his candidate.

Voters choose not only national and state officials, but also mayors and city councils. Farmers in the villages choose five neighbours to form a *panchayat*. A panchayat has one of the most important jobs in all India. With help from the national government

it gets the villagers together to build what they need. Sometimes they build a new road, sometimes a school, sometimes an irrigation ditch or well.

This is the India of your time: oxen pumping water from a well; dams that store water for electricity; aeroplanes and tonga carts; yak tails and isotopes.

What sort of life will Ram and Shalu and all the children of India have when they grow up? Part of the answer depends on friendly help they receive from people in other free countries. Part of the answer depends on you.

How to Pronounce Foreign Words in this Book

Word	Pronunciation	Word	Pronunciation
Afghanistan	af-*gan*-i-stan	Gandhi, Mahatma	*gahn*-dee ma-*hat*-ma
Allah	*al*-lah	Ganges	gan-jees
Allahabad	al-la-ha-bad	ghats	gahts
Arjuna	ar-*djuh*-nuh	gopis	*go*-pees
Aryan	air-ee-an		
		Hanuman	*hah*-nyou-mahn
Benares	ben-*ahr*-ess	Harijans	hair-ee-djans
Bengal	ben-*gahl*	Himalayas	him-al-*lay*-as
betel	*bay*-tell	Hindi	hin-dee
Bhagavad Gita	*bah*-dyou-a-vahd *gee*-tuh	Hindu	hin-du
		Holi	*ho*-lee
Bharata Natyam	bar-*at*-uh *nay*-tyam		
Bhave, Vinoba	bah-*vay*, veen-*oh*-buh	jaggery	*jag*-er-ee
Bhopal	boh-pahl	Jains	Janes
Bombay	*bom*-bay	Jaipur	*jeye*-poor
Brahma	*brah*-ma	Jhelum	*jeye*-lum
Brahmans	*brah*-muns	Jumna	*jum*-i-nuh
Buddha	*buh*-duh		
		Kabaddi	ka-bah-*dee*
Calcutta	cal-*cut*-tuh	Kashmir	kash-*meer*
chapati	ja-*pat*-ee	Krishna	*krish*-nuh
Cooch-Behar	koosh *bay*-har	Kurukshetra	*koor-uk-shay*-truh
dhoti	*doh*-tee	Ladakh	la-*dakh*
Divali	dee-*wahl*-ee	Lakshmi	*lahk*-shmay
Dravidians	drah-*vee*-dyans	Lok Sabha	lokh *sahb*-ha
Dussehra	du-*sair*-hruh		

Madras	mad-*rass*
maharajah	ma-*ha*-ra-jah
Mahavira	ma-*ha*-vee-hrah
Moghuls	mog-*ools*
Moslem	*moz*-lem
nabob	*naye*-bob
nawab	nuh-*wahb*
neem	neem
Nehru, Jawaharlal	*nay*-roo, *djah*-wah-*ha*-lahl
Nepal	*neh*-pahl
New Delhi	new *dell*-heye
Pakistan	Pah-ki-stan
panchayat	pahn-cheye-aht
Parsees	*pahr*-sees
peepul	*pee*-pul
phirans	*pee*-rans
Rajya Sabha	*radj*-ya sahb-ha
Rama	*rah*-muh
Ramayana	rah-meye-ya-nuh
Ramadan	*ram*-a-dan
Ravan	*rah*-van
roti	*roh*-tee
sadhus	sad-*ooz*
Saraswati	Sahr-uh-*swat*-ee
sari	*sah*-ree
Shah Jahan	shah *jah*-ha
Shalu	shall-*oo*
shikara	*shick*-a-ruh
Shiva	shee-*vah*
Sikh	seek
Sita	*see*-tuh
Srinigar	hsreen-i-gar
swamis	*swah*-mees
Tamil	*tah*-mil
Tibet	ti-*bet*
tonga	*tohm*-guh
Triveni	*triv*-ain-ee
Uchee-Zameen, Neechi-Zameen	*ootch*-ee *zahm*-een, *neetch*-ee *zahm*-een
Urdu	*uhr*-dyou
Vishnu	vish-nyou
Zoroastrianism	zoh-roh-*ass*-tree-an-izm

History

3rd millennium B.C.—Aryan Invasions.

2500 B.C.–1500 B.C.—Aryan civilization flourished.

327 B.C.–326 B.C.—Invasion of India by Alexander the Great.

566 B.C.–486 B.C.—Life of Gautama Buddha, founder of Buddhism.

273 B.C.–232 B.C.—Reign of King Asoka, who spread Buddhism throughout India and Far East.

A.D. 1192–1193—Moghul invasions reached climax in the fall of Delhi.

A.D. 1556–1605—Reign of Akbar the Great, famous Moghul emperor.

A.D. 1628–1658—Reign of Emperor Shan Jahan.

1632–1650—Building of the Taj Mahal by Shah Jahan.

1757—Battle of Plassey paves the way for British conquest of India.

1857—Indian mutiny put down; British tighten control.

October 2nd, 1869–January 30th, 1948—Life of Mahatma Gandhi, India's liberator.

August 15th, 1947—India wins independence and becomes a Dominion under a governor general.

January 26th, 1950—India becomes a sovereign Democratic Republic with Rajendra Prasad as first president.

1951—The first of India's five-year plans for industrialization and improvement of agriculture is inaugurated.

1957—Jawaharlal Nehru elected prime minister for the third successive term.

1960—Communist China attacks India's northern border.

Present—India begins third five-year plan, sets goals for wider education, continues development of electric power and irrigation projects, improvement of transport and farming methods.

Index